JBIOG
Josep
Klingel, Cynthia

Chief Joseph : chief of the Nez
Perce

CHIEF *Joseph*

SPIRIT
of America®

CHIEF *Joseph*

By Cynthia Klingel and Robert B. Noyed

The Child's World®
Chanhassen, Minnesota

6

CHIEF *Joseph*

Published in the United States of America by The Child's World®
PO Box 326 • Chanhassen, MN 55317-0326 • 800-599-READ • www.childsworld.com

Acknowledgments
The Child's World®: Mary Berendes, Publishing Director

Editorial Directions, Inc.: E. Russell Primm, Emily Dolbear, and Lucia Raatma, Editors; Linda S. Koutris, Photo Selector; Dawn Friedman, Photo Research; Red Line Editorial, Fact Research; Irene Keller, Copy Editor; Tim Griffin/IndexServ, Indexer; Chad Rubel, Proofreader

Photo
Cover: Christie's Images/Corbis; Museum of the City of New York, NY/Scala/Art Resource, NY: 13 top; Smithsonian American Art Museum, Washington, DC/Art Resource, NY: 14, 26; Bridgeman Art Library: 6; Corbis: 24; Bettmann/Corbis: 15, 27; Christie's Images/Corbis: 2; Dave G. Houser/Corbis: 11; Layne Kennedy/Corbis: 7; Medford Historical Society Collection/Corbis: 19; Peter Turnley/Corbis: 10, 21; Hulton Archive/Getty Images: 9; Library of Congress: 17; National Museum of the American Indian, Smithsonian Institution, (#N33738), photo by Maj. Lee Moorhouse: 28; North Wind Picture Archives: 8, 12, 18, 20; Stock Montage: 13 bottom, 22, 23, 25.

Registration
The Child's World®, Spirit of America®, and their associated logos are the sole property and registered trademarks of The Child's World®.

Library of Congress Cataloging-in-Publication Data
Klingel, Cynthia Fitterer.
  Chief Joseph : chief of the Nez Percé / by Cynthia Klingel and Robert B. Noyed.
    p. cm.
Includes bibliographical references.
Summary: A brief introduction to the life of Chief Joseph, who fought to keep the Oregon land that his people had lived on for generations.
  ISBN 1-56766-165-3 (Library Bound : alk. paper)
 1. Joseph, Nez Percé chief, 1840–1904—Juvenile literature. 2. Nez Percé Indians—Biography—Juvenile literature. [1. Joseph, Nez Percé chief, 1840–1904. 2. Nez Percé Indians—Biography. 3. Indians of North America—Northwest, Pacific—Biography. 4. Kings, queens, rulers, etc.]
I. Noyed, Robert B. II. Title.
  E99.N5 J586 2003
  979.004'9741'0092—dc21

                    2001007398

14 20 28

Contents

Chapter ONE

Joseph the Younger

LONG BEFORE **COLONISTS** SETTLED IN AMERICA, Native American tribes lived there. They built their homes and set up their governments. Throughout U.S. history, however, white settlers forced many of these tribes to leave their land.

Throughout U.S. history, white settlers fought for land that Native Americans had lived on for centuries.

Some Native American leaders fought to keep their land and defend their people. Chief Joseph spent his entire life defending the rights of his people—the Nez Percé.

Chief Joseph was born in 1840. He was born in the Wallowa Valley of what is now north-eastern Oregon. His father was the chief

of the Nez Percé tribe in that area. Chief Joseph was given the Indian name *Hin-mah-too-yah-lat-kekt*. This name means "thunder rolling down the mountain."

His father was known as Joseph the **Elder**. Joseph the Elder took the name Joseph when he was **baptized** in 1838. Chief Joseph's father was one of the first of the Nez Percé to become a **Christian**. He also supported the tribe's peaceful relationship with white people.

Hin-mah-too-yah-lat-kekt was also known as Joseph or Joseph the Younger. When he was about five years old, Joseph the Younger

Chief Joseph was born in the Wallowa Valley in Oregon.

7

went to school. White **missionaries** ran the school. He loved school and he loved to play, too. Joseph's father often reminded him that he would be the next person to lead the tribe.

In 1847, trouble came to the white missionaries. A sickness killed many members of the Cayuse, a tribe of Indians who lived near the Nez Percé. The Cayuse people blamed the white missionaries for bringing the disease. The Cayuse killed 12 of the white missionaries.

The Cayuse Indians killed 12 missionaries in 1847.

The U.S. Army was sent to fight the Cayuse people. Many of the white missionaries left the area. Joseph the Elder watched the white missionaries leaving. He said, "Perhaps the white religion is not so strong after all. When trouble comes, the missionaries' faith is in their feet rather than their hearts."

Several years went by. Joseph the Elder and his family were no longer Christians. They returned to the religion of their own people. They called the Earth their mother and loved the land.

When he was about 10 years old, Joseph the Younger went off to pray to the Great Spirit. All young men of the tribe pray to the Great Spirit at this age. As he prayed, he saw a vision of himself as a great chief. He heard a voice give him the name Thunder Rolling down the Mountain.

At first, the voice frightened Joseph. He prayed for the courage to live up to his new name. Joseph was learning the wisdom it would take to be a strong leader.

Chief Joseph about 1900

9

TODAY, NEZ PERCÉ PEOPLE LIVE ALL OVER THE WORLD. MANY NEZ PERCÉ families still live on or near the Nez Perce Reservation in Idaho (below).

The people of the Nez Percé tribe are modern in every way, but their traditions are still important to them. The tribe's older people, or elders, teach the younger people the old ways of the tribe. The elders pass on the tribe's language, beliefs, foods, and dances by telling stories.

The Nez Percé hold traditional celebrations throughout the year. For days, the people enjoy dancing, singing, and eating. Many Nez Percé wear colorful ceremonial clothing at these celebrations (left).

Today's Nez Percé wear modern clothing and live in modern houses. They work in many professions.

The beliefs that guide the Nez Percé people, and their strong ties to the Earth and nature, are many hundreds of years old. This link to their heritage remains a key to their culture today.

Chapter Two

Becoming a Chief

Chief Joseph learned to hunt deer in the mountains of Oregon.

As the years went by, Joseph the Younger learned more and more from his father. He learned how to be a great hunter and warrior. Like his father, he worried about keeping the tribe's land.

More and more white people were moving onto Nez Percé land. The white settlers chopped down trees, built fences across age-old Indian trails, and took over Indian land. Some settlers even gave liquor to

the Indians and then cheated them out of their land. Joseph the Elder hoped that his tribe's peaceful relationship with the white people would continue.

Families of settlers traveled through the West—and over Indian land.

In 1855, Joseph the Elder helped the governor of Oregon Territory set up a **reservation** for the Nez Percé tribe. The reservation included land in Oregon and in parts of Idaho. The tribe promised to live only on the land in the Wallowa Valley.

A government leader meeting with the Nez Percé in 1857

In return, the U.S. government promised to give food, money, and supplies to the Nez Percé. The government kept its promise with the Nez Percé for only a few years.

In 1863, many more white settlers came to the area searching for gold. The government took back almost all of the 6 million acres (2.4 million hectares) of land it had given to the Nez Percé. Now the government wanted the tribe to live on a small piece of land in Idaho. Joseph the Elder, his son, and other members of the tribe were very upset.

Joseph the Elder refused to move his people from the Wallowa Valley. He also refused to sign the **treaty** with the U.S. government.

The white settlers and gold miners took the land that had been given to the tribe by the government. Although most of the Nez Percé people were friendly, the settlers called them "savages." The settlers believed that the tribe had no right to the land.

In time, white settlers in search of gold took over Indian land.

14

In 1871, Joseph the Elder was dying. He called for his son. He told his son, "Your time has come. Now you will be the chief of these people. They look up to you to guide them. You must stop your ears if the white men ask you to sign a treaty and sell your home. A few more years and the white men will be all around you. They have their eyes on this land. But never forget my dying words! This country holds your father's body. Never sell the bones of your father and mother."

Joseph the Younger became Chief Joseph in 1871.

A short time later, Joseph the Elder died. His son became chief of the Nez Percé. He was now called Chief Joseph. He was very sad about his father's death. He was committed to keeping his people on the land in the Wallowa Valley.

Interesting Fact

▶ Both men and women of the Nez Percé paint their faces for special ceremonies.

BEFORE THE TREATIES WITH WHITE PEOPLE, THE NEZ PERCÉ lived in Oregon, Washington, and Idaho. They were a traveling people. They often lived in small villages. The villages were usually along the banks of a stream or river.

The people in the village were related to one another. They consisted of a family of grandparents, aunts and uncles, sons and daughters, and their families. These are now called extended families.

During the cold winter months, the people of the village lived in homes called longhouses. These were sometimes 100 feet (31 m) long. Several families lived together in a longhouse. A row of fire pits, or hearths, ran down the center of the long-house. At other times of the year, these houses were used for ceremonies or special occasions.

The Nez Percé ate a variety of foods. They enjoyed salmon and other fish from the rivers. They also hunted large animals, such as deer, elk, moose, and bear. The women dug up roots and collected plants. They collected many kinds of berries and nuts.

Their clothing was made from the skins of the animals they hunted. The men wore long shirts, leggings, moccasins, and wrapped themselves in breechcloths (right). Women wore long dresses and moccasins. Their dresses were often beautifully decorated with colorful designs, animal teeth, and beads.

Chapter THREE

Broken Promises

AS THE NEW LEADER OF THE NEZ PERCÉ, Chief Joseph had a difficult job. He knew he would have to cooperate with the U.S. government. He also had to keep his promise to his father. He had to defend the tribe's land.

Chief Joseph resisted the government's orders to move to the small reservation in

Homes on the reservation in Lapwai, Idaho, in the 1870s

Idaho. In 1873, the government gave Chief Joseph and his people permission to stay on their land. All white settlers had to leave the Wallowa Valley. It seemed like good news for the Nez Percé. Unfortunately, the government changed its mind.

Government **officials** came to make a new treaty with Chief Joseph. They told Chief Joseph to move his people north to a new reservation. But Chief Joseph was committed to keeping his tribe on the land. He told the government leaders, "This land is our mother. We cannot leave her." The government leaders promised Chief Joseph that the tribe would get new land in the north.

Chief Joseph refused to sign the treaty. He knew that the government usually broke such promises. He had no reason to trust the government.

In May 1877, the U.S. Army came to Wallowa Valley. They had orders to force the Nez Percé tribe to move to the new land. The army, led by General Oliver Otis Howard, threatened to attack the tribe if they did not move.

General Oliver Otis Howard and his troops were sent to force the Nez Percé off their land in 1877.

19

Interesting Fact

▶ Every permanent Nez Percé village had a round sweathouse. This building was used for cleanliness of the body and spirit.

Chief Joseph knew that many warriors in his tribe were ready to fight. He wanted to avoid war and urged his people to leave the area. Even though members of the tribe were sad and angry, they moved out of the Wallowa Valley to their new land.

Shortly after leaving the valley, the tribe made camp at night. Chief Joseph saw that a small number of young men wanted to fight for their land. Even though the chief tried to stop them, the young warriors left camp and attacked white settlers. They killed four white men. When they returned to the camp, they said to Chief Joseph, "Now you will have to fight with us. Soon the soldiers will be here. Prepare for war!"

For years, Chief Joseph had worked for peace. But he knew that the army would soon attack and he would have to lead his people.

U.S. troops prepare to fight the Nez Percé.

THE NEZ PERCE National Historical Park has 38 sites. These sites are in Idaho, Oregon, Washington, and Montana. They are meant to remind people of the legends of the Nez Percé tribe.

The sites are related to events in the lives of the Nez Percé and the explorers, fur traders, missionaries, soldiers, settlers, gold miners, and farmers who were once in the area. The valleys, mountains, and prairies in the park sites represent the area that was home to the Nez Percé tribe.

The park has two visitor centers. One is at the park's headquarters in Spalding, Idaho. The other visitor center is at Big Hole National Battlefield, near Wisdom, Montana. It is open all year. Staff there can answer questions about the history of the Nez Percé people. Exhibits and guided tours are also available.

Both visitor centers have Junior Ranger programs for children between 5 and 12 years old. They offer children an opportunity to learn more about the park and the Nez Percé people.

Chapter FOUR

"I Will Fight No More Forever"

SOON THE ARMY BEGAN TO ATTACK CHIEF Joseph's tribe. The Nez Percé had only about 200 warriors, but they were fierce fighters. In the first battle, the Nez Percé crushed the army troops at White Bird Canyon.

Soldiers attack Chief Joseph and his tribe of about 700 people.

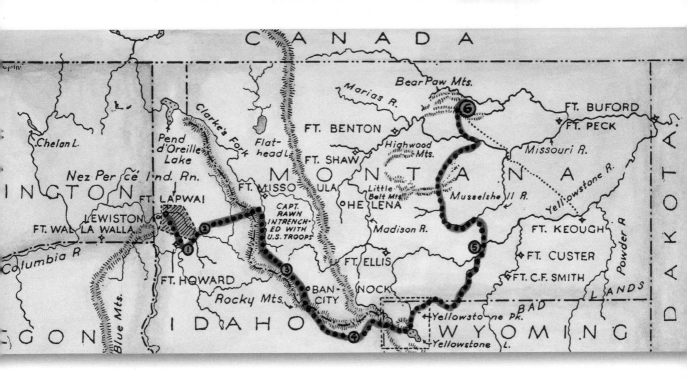

Chief Joseph and the other tribe leaders led the attack against the army. In the three months that followed, the small band of Nez Percé warriors fought U.S. troops in several battles. The army troops were pushed back and Chief Joseph led his people on a march of 1,400 miles (2,253 kilometers).

The Nez Percé won fight after fight. But Chief Joseph knew that his people had to escape. It was only a matter of time before the army would take over his tribe.

Each time the tribe tried to escape, the army trapped them. The warriors were then forced to fight another battle. They continued to win these battles, though.

In 1877, Chief Joseph led women, children, and warriors east to escape U.S. troops.

Interesting Fact

▶ The name "Nez Percé" comes from two French words meaning "pierced nose." Actually, few Nez Percé people ever had pierced noses. A French explorer who saw some people wearing shells in their noses (as a decoration) gave the tribe that name.

A Nez Percé chief on horseback in 1877

People all over the United States read about the battles in the newspapers. Chief Joseph was known for his skill in leading his warriors and his concern for the Nez Percé children and elders.

For almost four months, the Nez Percé traveled and tried to escape the army. Finally, just 30 miles (48 km) from the Canadian border, the soldiers surrounded Chief Joseph and his people. It was the end, and Chief Joseph was forced to **surrender**.

On October 5, 1877, Chief Joseph rode alone to surrender to the army generals. He gave his rifle to the generals. Chief Joseph gave a memorable speech. He said, "I am tired of fighting. Our chiefs are killed. . . . It is cold and we have no blankets. The little

*When Chief Joseph finally
surrendered to the U.S.
Army, he gave a sad and
passionate speech.*

This bronze coin of Chief Joseph was created in 1889. It is the only known portrait of him that was made while he was alive.

children are freezing. We have no food. Hear me, my chiefs. I am tired. My heart is sick and sad. From where the sun now stands, I will fight no more forever." The leaders of the U.S. government promised Chief Joseph that he and his people could return to their land in the Wallowa Valley. But once again, the government broke its promise. Chief Joseph and the Nez Percé people were sent to an Indian reservation near what is now the state of Oklahoma. Many of the Nez Percé people died of diseases on that reservation.

In 1879, Chief Joseph made a trip to Washington, D.C., to meet with President

Rutherford B. Hayes. He tried to convince President Hayes to let his people return to their land in the Wallowa Valley in Oregon.

In 1885, the Nez Percé were allowed to return to that part of the country. But many members of the tribe, including Chief Joseph, were separated from the rest of their people. They were taken to a reservation in northern Washington instead.

President Rutherford B. Hayes

Chief Joseph spent the rest of his life working for fair treatment for his people. He wanted the U.S. government to keep its promises to the Nez Percé. But Chief Joseph died before achieving his dream. He died on the Nez Percé reservation in northern Washington on September 21, 1904.

Chief Joseph will be remembered for his desire for peace and for his courage. He will also be known for leading his people's struggle to stay on their land.

Chief Joseph in traditional clothes

1840 Chief Joseph is born in the Wallowa Valley in Oregon.

1855 Joseph the Elder helps the governor of Oregon Territory set up a reservation for the Nez Percé tribe.

1863 After the U.S. government takes back land it had given to the Nez Percé, Joseph the Elder refuses to move his people from the Wallowa Valley. He also refuses to sign a treaty with the U.S. government.

1871 Joseph the Elder dies. Joseph the Younger becomes chief of the Nez Percé.

1873 The U.S. government gives Chief Joseph and his people permission to stay on their land.

1877 The U.S. Army comes to Wallowa Valley with orders to force the Nez Percé tribe to new land. Chief Joseph leads his people on a march to the north that lasts almost four months.

1879 Chief Joseph goes to Washington, D.C., to meet with President Rutherford B. Hayes. He asks for the return of his people's land.

1885 The Nez Percé are allowed to return to Wallowa Valley.

1904 Chief Joseph dies on a reservation in northern Washington, separated from the rest of his people.

baptized (BAP-tyzed)
When people are baptized to become Christians, they are sprinkled with water during a ceremony. Chief Joseph's father was baptized in 1838.

Christian (KRISS-chuhn)
A Christian is a person who believes in Jesus Christ and follows his teachings. Chief Joseph's father was a Christian.

colonists (KOL-uh-nists)
Colonists are people who live in a newly settled area. Native Americans lived in America long before colonists arrived from other lands.

elder (EL-dur)
An elder is someone who is older. Chief Joseph's father was known as Joseph the Elder.

missionaries (MISH-uh-NER-eez)
Missionaries are people sent by a church to teach others about their religion. Missionaries ran the first school Chief Joseph attended.

officials (of-FISH-uhlz)
Officials are people who have important jobs in an organization. Chief Joseph did not trust many government officials.

reservation (rez-ur-VAY-shuhn)
A reservation is land set aside by the government for Native American tribes. In 1855, a reservation was set up for the Nez Percé tribe.

surrender (suh-REN-dur)
To surrender means to give up or admit defeat in a battle. Chief Joseph was finally forced to surrender to U.S. soldiers.

treaty (TREE-tee)
A treaty is an agreement between two governments. Joseph the Elder refused to sign a treaty with the U.S. government.

For Further INFORMATION

Web Sites

Visit our homepage for lots of links about Chief Joseph as well as the Nez Percé:
http://www.childsworld.com/links.html

Note to Parents, Teachers, and Librarians:
We routinely verify our Web links to make sure they're safe,
active sites—so encourage your readers to check them out!

Books

Fox, Mary Virginia. *Chief Joseph of the Nez Perce Indians: Champion of Liberty.*
Chicago: Childrens Press, 1993.

Sanford, William Reynolds. *Chief Joseph: Nez Perce Warrior.* Springfield, N.J.:
Enslow Publishers, 1994.

Taylor, Marian W. *Chief Joseph: Nez Perce Leader.* New York: Chelsea House, 1993.

Places to Visit or Contact

Wallowa Band Nez Perce Trail Interpretive Center, Inc.
To find out about Nez Percé culture and history
P. O. Box 15
Wallowa, OR 97885
541-886-3101

Nez Perce National Historical Park
To get information about visiting the park
39063 U.S. Highway 95
Spalding, ID 83540-9715
208-843-2261

Index